Bon Appetit!

Shawnee Hunter Georges Drouillard's List of Fine Dining Establishments along the Lewis and Clark Trail, as of A.D. 1806

and

The Life and Times of Georges P. Drouillard

Historian Richard M. Gaffney, M.A.

Bloomington, IN   authorHOUSE®   Milton Keynes, UK

AuthorHouse™
1663 Liberty Drive, Suite 200
Bloomington, IN 47403
www.authorhouse.com
Phone: 1-800-839-8640

AuthorHouse™ *UK Ltd.*
500 Avebury Boulevard
Central Milton Keynes, MK9 2BE
www.authorhouse.co.uk
Phone: 08001974150

© 2006 Historian Richard M. Gaffney, M.A.. All rights reserved.

No part of this book may be reproduced, stored in a retrieval system, or transmitted by any means without the written permission of the author.

First published by AuthorHouse 9/5/2006

ISBN: 1-4259-5123-6 (sc)

Library of Congress Control Number: 2006907278

Printed in the United States of America
Bloomington, Indiana

This book is printed on acid-free paper.

Includes bibliographical references.

1. Fine dining establishments along the Lewis and Clark Trail in Missouri.
2. Georges Drouillard, 1770-1810, limited biographical material.
3. Indians of North America—Wars—1750-1815.
4. Shawnee Nation and Chief Kishkalwa's Band, Migration to Missouri.
5. George Drouillard's Signatures, a comparison.
6. Bicentennial of Lewis and Clark Expedition, 2006, Monument to members.

May God Bless America

Shawnee Hunter and Interpreter Georges P. Drouillard, as portrayed by Re-enactor Richard M. Gaffney, M.A.
(Color Photo by David V. Gaffney.)

Bon Appetit!

Shawnee Hunter Georges Drouillard's List of Fine Dining Establishments along the Lewis and Clark Trail, as of A.D. 1806

and

The Life and Times of Georges P. Drouillard

Being a compilation of what we have learned in recent historical studies.

With space for the readers to take notes on their own
Fine dining adventures along the Lewis and Clark Trail,
By

Historian Richard M. Gaffney, M.A.,
A.D. 2006

Stone marker on grounds of Fort Massac, now an Illinois State Park, erected in November, 2003, to commemorate the 200th Anniversary of when Captains Lewis and Clark met Shawnee hunter Georges Drouillard, who eventually agreed to accompany the Corps of Northwestern Discovery on the expedition up the Missouri River.
(Photo by Richard M. Gaffney.)

To the Glory of Almighty God,
Father, Son, and Great Spirit,
and
To my late mother and father,
who would have been very proud of me,
had they lived to see this day.
--Georges

Model for the statue of Georges Drouillard being made for the Bicentennial Monument to be erected on the grounds of the State Capitol in Jefferson City, Mo. The monument will include heroic size figures of Capt. Lewis, Seaman, Capt. Clark, and York, as well as the one of Drouillard, who represents the Missourians, mostly of French Canadian and Native American stock, who went on the expedition. The sculptor, Sabra Tull Meyer, stands beside the unfinished figure of Drouillard.
(Photo by Jamie Meyer, son of the sculptor, 2006.)

Table of Contents

Part I   1
Shawnee Hunter Georges Drouillard's List of Fine Dining Establishments Along the Lewis and Clark Trail, As of A.D. 1806

Part II   55
The Life and Times of Georges P. Drouillard by Historian Richard M Gaffney, M.A.

Chapter 1   57
Early Life and Education of Georges P. Drouillard

Chapter 2   71
Chief Kishkalwa and Moving to Missouri

Chapter 3   81
Study of Drouillard's Signature

Chapter 4   93
How "Drewyer" Is Being Remembered

Part III   103
Bon Appetit! and The Life and Times of Georges P. Drouillard by Historian Richard M. Gaffney. M.A.

Acknowledgements   105
About the Author   107
Also by Richard M. Gaffney   110
Information about the Shawnees   112
About the Book   115

Table of Illustrations

Cover, The Indian Hunter and Canoe

(Photo by Malcolm Waskiewics.)

Shawnee Hunter and Interpreter Georges P. Drouillard, as portrayed by Re-enactor Richard M. Gaffney, M.A.

(Color Photo by David V. Gaffney.) vi

Stone marker on grounds of Fort Massac, now an Illinois State Park, erected in November, 2003, to commemorate the 200th Anniversary of when Captains Lewis and Clark met Shawnee hunter Georges Drouillard, who eventually agreed to accompany the Corps of Northwestern Discovery on the expedition up the Missouri River.

(Photo by Richard M. Gaffney.) viii

Model for the statue of Georges Drouillard being made for the Bicentennial Monument to be erected on the grounds of the State Capitol in Jefferson City, Mo. The monument will include heroic size figures of Capt. Lewis, Seaman, Capt. Clark, and York, as well as the one of Drouillard, who represents the Missourians, mostly of French Canadian and Native American stock, who went on the expedition. The sculptor, Sabra Tull Meyer, stands beside the unfinished figure of Drouillard.

(Photo by Jamie Meyer, son of the sculptor, 2006.) x

Shawnee hunter and interpreter Georges P. Drouillard, as portrayed by re-enactor Richard M. Gaffney, M.A.

(Photo by David V. Gaffney.) xvi

"Here's Looking at You!" Face-on view of unfinished model of statue of Georges P. Drouillard, by Sculptor Sabra Tull Meyer of Missouri.

(Photo at foundry by Jamie Meyer, 2006.) 54

Map I. Map showing western land claims of the 13 Colonies that became States, as of the Year 1783.

(By the author.) 56

Map II. The territory of the 13 colonies, showing the Proclamation Line of 1763, drawn along the watershed of the Appalachian Mountain chain, and Indian Lands. (Major Indian nations shown, some on both sides of the line.)

(By the author.) 62

Portrait of Chief Kishkalwa, about 1825. He moved his people from what now is Ohio across what now are Indiana and Illinois, and across the Mississippi River into what now is Missouri, during the years 1782-1797. This portrait by artist Charles Bird King probably was painted during the chief's visit to Washington, D.C., in 1825, some 40 years after leading his people away from the "bloody Americans."

(Source: Moore, Robert, NATIVE AMERICANS, 1997.) 70

Map III. The vicinity of Cape Girardeau, circa 1800, showing Shawnee settlements. (Modern county lines added in Missouri to assist the reader. Map by the author, 2006, not drawn to scale; width of rivers exaggerated purposely, courses approximate. Area of Spanish land grant to the Shawnees is only approximate, as are locations of Shawnee villages.)

Sources include Denny and Harlan, Atlas of Lewis and Clark in Missouri; Warren, The Shawnees and their Neighbors, Jackson, "Cape Girardeau and the Corps of Discovery," and other writings. 73

Depiction of a Shawnee man of the Apple Creek settlement in Upper Louisiana, as contained in Houck's A History of Missouri, 1908, citing the artist and the source.

By Warin (from A History of Missouri, by Louis Houck, 1908. 75

The Signing of the Treaty. This sculpture was designed by Karl Bitter for the 1904 World's Fair in St. Louis, known as the Louisiana Purchase Centennial Exposition. After the Fair, it was brought to Jefferson City for permanent display. It depicts Robert Livingston, standing, left, and James Monroe, seated, for the United States, and François Barbé-Marbois, signing, for France, 1803. By the treaty, the U.S.A. acquired Louisiana Territory from France for $15,000,000. The Treaty sculpture faces the north front of the Missouri State Capitol.

(Photo by the author, 2006.) 78

Enhanced image of the signature of "G.P. DrouiLLard's" presumably made in 1804 on the soft limestone or dolomite of Bull Rock, a bluff face on the right bank of the Missouri River upstream of Jefferson City, Mo.

(Image courtesy of Mr. Quentin Wade, Cole County, Mo.)   82

Copy of a Promissory Note for $301.63 and 1/3 from Georges Drouillard to Frederick Graeter, dated 11 February, 1804, at Fort Massac, showing his signature. The witness's name is Antoine Lasselle.

(From the Manuel Lisa Papers, courtesy of the Missouri Historical Society, St. Louis, Mo., Rocheport),   84

Copy of Promissory Note to Alexander McNeir, 30 April, 1807.

(From the Bates Family Papers, courtesy of the Missouri Historical Society, St. Louis, Mo.)   86

Copy of a Promissory Note for $19 from Georges Drouillard to Joseph Kimball, dated 25 March, 1809, at Bellefontaine, Mo.

(From the Fur Trade Collection, courtesy of the Missouri Historical Society, St. Louis, Mo.)   88

Copy of an excerpt from a faded original of a legal deposition given by Georges Drouillard, dated 26 April, 1809, in St. Louis, showing Drouillard's signature. Note the old-style "long-tailed s" used in the script on this document.

(From the Manuel Lisa Papers, courtesy of the Missouri Historical Society, St. Louis, Mo.)   90

Photo of a Maquette of the Lewis and Clark Bicentennial Capitol Monument by sculptor Sabra Tull Meyer, 2006, showing the Corps of Discovery figures (l-r) of York, Capt. Lewis, Seaman, Capt. Clark, and Georges Drouillard.

(Photo by Col. John Tandy.)   94

Shawnee Hunter and Interpreter Georges P. Drouillard, as portrayed by Historian Richard M. Gaffney, during the 2004 re-enactment of the start of the expedition from Camp DuBois, Mississippi River. The Missouri shoreline is in the distance. Crew members of the Discovery Expedition of St. Charles are shown.

(Photo by Gerald D. Manchester.) 97

Shawnee Hunter and Interpreter Georges P. Drouillard in Hunting Camp with flintlock short rifle, pack basket, canoe paddle, and shelter tarp as portrayed by Historian R.M. Gaffney.

(Color photo by Dolores White Dove Gaffney, Cherokee.) 102

George P. Drouillard (portrayed by R.M. Gaffney) and White Dove (Mrs. Dolores Gaffney), on the grounds of Locust Grove, east of Louisville, Ky., autumn, 2003, at the time of the Falls of the Ohio signature event of the Lewis and Clark Bicentennial Commemoration.

(Photo by Gerald D. Manchester.) 109

Shawnee hunter and interpreter Georges P. Drouillard, as portrayed by re-enactor Richard M. Gaffney, M.A.
(Photo by David V. Gaffney.)

Part I

Bon Appetít!

Shawnee Hunter
Georges Drouillard's
List of Fine Dining Establishments
along the Lewis and Clark Trail,
as of A.D. 1806

Updated by
Richard M. Gaffney, M.A.,
A.D. 2006

Introduction

Everyone must eat to live. Many of us live to eat, or at least we want to enjoy each meal. Sometimes, as we journey through life, busy with hard work, it is necessary to be satisfied with whatever we can get quickly, by the wayside.

We call that, "fast food," and frequently, we are disappointed in both the quality of the food, and the *ambience* of the restaurant. However, even "trailside" food can be tasty, wholesome, and served in pleasant surroundings. Our level of satisfaction or appreciation often has a lot to do with our level of expectations.

When we have the time to enjoy good food, in a pleasant atmosphere, with amiable company, most of us prefer fine dining experiences. In 1806, there were no fine dining establishments along the Missouri River, the Lewis and Clark Trail on their Voyage of Northwest Discovery.

The reader will discover that there are, in 2006, a number of fine dining establishments that Shawnee Hunter Georges Drouillard ("Drewyer") would have really enjoyed—places that Lewis and Clark Bicentennial re-enactors have discovered and recommend to you, so that you may better enjoy the journey of the Bicentennial of the Expedition.

The following blank pages in this guidebook are for the use of the readers in taking notes on their own fine dining experiences along the Missouri River. The printed pages are your guide to some of the best dining to be found along the Lewis and Clark Trail in Missouri. Read on! Take notes! Let the journey begin!

Bon Appetit!

In Part II, the reader will learn more about George "Drewyer," the master hunter and interpreter who went along with Captain Lewis and Captain Clark as a civilian within the military expedition, and was accorded the privileges of a member of the officer corps.

Learn more about the remarkable man who has long been virtually ignored by historians, or relegated to the category of "Frenchman" or "French-Canadian" (he was neither), as if he were merely one of the hired boatmen.

Come, follow his journey across the continent and across the years.

Bon Appetit!
St. Charles, Mo.

May 16-21, A.D. 1804
Sept. 21, A.D. 1806

(Eventually became the first State Capital city, and the first legislative chambers can still be visited. This is the home of the Discovery Expedition of St. Charles. The keelboat and the pirogues used in the Bicentennial re-enactment are stored in the Boat House at the Lewis and Clark Center, by the Missouri River. The annual Lewis and Clark Rendezvous is held the third weekend in May. Historic Main Street retains its 18th and early 19th Century atmosphere and delights visitors. This is the eastern terminus of the Katy Trail State Park, and of the old Boone's Lick Road established by Daniel Boone and his sons. St. Charles is the seat of St. Charles County.)

Bon Appetít!
Washington, Mo.

May 25, A.D. 1804
Sept. 20, A.D. 1806

Bon Appetit!
Hermann, Mo.

May 27, A.D. 1804
Sept. 20, A.D. 1806

Bon Appetit!

City of Jefferson, Mo.

June 3-4, A.D. 1804
Sept. 19, A.D. 1806

(This site was laid out by order of the State Legislature to be the State Capital city, to be halfway across the state, and to be along the Missouri River, the principal route of travel in the early 19th Century. The State Capitol Building which visitors see is the third, the earlier buildings having been lost to fires. See the Jefferson Landing State Historic Site at the northern end of Jefferson Street, they and the city having been named for the President who purchased the Louisiana Territory in 1803. The Capitol Building was designed to resemble the national Capitol Building, and the interior is one of the most beautiful of all the state capitols. Visitors may take tours of the building all through the week, and see the historic paintings and sculptures therein. Included are statues of Thomas Jefferson, Meriwether Lewis, and William Clark, in addition to busts of Sacagawea and famous Missourians. Coming in 2007 is a Lewis and Clark Bicentennial Commemorative Monument on a site in a park located just east of the Capitol Building. It will contain five heroic size figures: Capt. Lewis; his dog, Seaman; Capt. Clark; his manservant, York, and Georges Drouillard, the civilian hunter and interpreter, who represents the Missourians who went on the Expedition of Discovery, and later helped to open the Fur Trade in the Rocky Mountain West.)

Bon Appetit!

Kaullen Mercantile Company ~ circa 1895
National Register of Historic Places

Bring your 21st Century tastes into this restored marvelous 19th Century building for lunch or dinner. The ambience offers "instant nostalgia" to those who appreciate the authenticity of the architecture of the "gay '90s."

Opened in 2003, O'Donoghue's offers a wide variety of appetizers, entrées, salads, breads, and desserts. While steaks and seafood are featured, one can always find delicious chicken, pork, ham, and pasta on the menu. Adult beverages are also available.

Reasonable prices, excellent quality, congenial atmosphere, and wide selection are yours from 11:00 A.M., Monday through Saturday. During pleasant weather, fresh air dining is offered on the deck.

For lunch, hot or cold sandwiches are featured, and carryouts are available. Ask for reservations for large parties. Call 573:635-1332. Visit 900-902 East High Street, Jefferson City, Mo. You'll be pleased that you did. Georges would have liked it, here.

Bon Appetit!

The Capital City Steakhouse proudly serves only certified Angus beef at its 127-129 East High Street dining rooms. Poultry, pork, seafood, and pasta dishes also are available on their extensive quality menu. There are dinner and luncheon menus.

A newly remodeled banquet room can be reserved, and special events can be catered upon request. Be sure to call 573:893-3888 well in advance of your event to assure booking.

A wide variety of beverages is available, as well as soups and salads. The restaurant in the heart of the central business district, close to the State Capitol, is open for fine dining from 11:00 A.M., Mondays through Fridays, and after 4:00 P.M., Saturdays. Georges would have liked it, here.

Bon Appetit!

Georges Drouillard never tasted wienerschnitzel so good! Or try the chicken Kiev with all the fixings! This is food that is cooked right, the "old country" way, and served right, too. You may never have experienced Old World excellence, like this.

Salads, fresh breads, adult beverages, and desserts round out the large number of selections on the menu. They have had the same good cook for 22 years! For an old-time German ambience, you can't beat Das Stein Haus!

The flags of the U.S.A., Austria, Switzerland, and Germany fly here. Inside, there is a gift shop with German Christmas tree ornaments and steins for sale. German music plays softly in the background for your dining pleasure. You can relax at Das Stein Haus.

Bon Appetit!

Come visit the old wine cellar at Das Haus of Europe at 623 East High Street in Jefferson City.

Open Tuesdays through Fridays from 4:00 P.M., one can experience the ambience of old Germany. This place has the same owner as Das Stein Haus, and the excellent quality also is the same.

Skoal!

Bon Appetít!

Mel's Country Café,

2421 Industrial Drive, Jefferson City, MO 65109,

Dial 573:893-9115.

For "down home" good recipes, appreciated by all generations, it's hard to beat Mel's Country Café! Soup of the day, salad, and country fried steak are available every day.

There are daily specials at reasonable prices, and senior citizens should be sure to ask for their discount. The broasted chicken is great.

One of the most popular dining spots in the capital city, Mel's has a convivial atmosphere, attractive and wholesome.

Be sure to have a piece of pie or a dish of cobbler before heading for home. Georges Drouillard would have!

Bon Appetit!

Rocheport, Mo.

7 June, A.D. 1804
19 September, A.D. 1806

(In the *Journals* of Lewis and Clark, we read, "*...brackfasst at the Mouth of a large creek...called big Monetou...a Short distance about the mouth of this Creek, is Several Courious Paintings and Carveings in the projecting rock of Limestone inlade with white red and blue flint, of a verry good quality, the Indians have taken of this flint great quantities.*" The petroglyphs and pictographs on the rock bluffs, called Big Manitou Bluffs, have been lost, partly due to the construction of a railroad in the 19th Century. At Rocheport, founded in 1825, is the only tunnel on that railroad, now used as part of the Katy Trail State Park (mile marker 178.3). There also is a Rocheport Museum and Riverfront Trail in this historic city that still has the atmosphere of the steamboat days of the late 1800s. It is listed on the National Register of Historic Places.)

Bon Appetit!

Fine dining can be expressed in numerous ways. In Rocheport, the Trailside Café is situated alongside the old M-K-T Railroad grade, now the Katy Trail State Park. This follows the Lewis and Clark Trail, which, of course, is the Missouri River.

Trailside food, when you have a choice of outdoor dining or air conditioned comfort, and when you have a choice of buffalo burgers or a wide variety of domestic meat sandwiches, such as ham, turkey, beef, grilled chicken, or pork tenderloin in pleasant surroundings, can surpass the ambience and cuisine of a high-falootin' restaurant.

Georges Drouillard would have enjoyed the Trailside Café, a business which is a member of the Mid-Missouri Manitou Bluffs Chapter of the Lewis and Clark Trail Heritage Foundation. They offer breakfast, lunch, dinner, and snacks to friends and weary travelers.

Historian Richard M. Gaffney, M.A.

The great-grandfather of Proprietor Larry Horning spent the night at Rocheport in 1839, on his way upriver on a steamboat. The family later returned to settle down here. Don't forget to stop in and get some of the best ice cream on the Lewis and Clark Trail!

Bon Appetit!
Boonville, Mo.

June 8, A.D. 1804
September 19, A.D. 1806

Bon Appetit!
Arrow Rock, Mo.

June 9, A.D. 1804

(Renowned as a principal eastern terminus of the Santa Fé Trail and of the Oregon Trail, historic Arrow Rock was named for the flint quarried by the Native People for their spear and arrow points in prehistoric times. A drive through old Arrow Rock is a step back into the 1830s, complete with wooden sidewalks and stone paving. The Lyceum Theater is a summer favorite for plays and musicals, but this is an all-season town, and now has a Lewis and Clark Bicentennial Trail down to the Missouri River landing. Part of Arrow Rock is a Missouri State Park with museum exhibits, and the historic old Huston Tavern.)

Bon Appetit!

Historic Arrow Rock Tavern
"Oldest Continuous Operating Restaurant West of The Mississippi Since 1834"

302 Main Street
P. O. Box 23
Arrow Rock, Missouri 65320

Mike & Mary Duncan   660-837-3200
Proprietors   www.arrowrocktavern.com

Georges Drouillard would have felt right at home in this historic town on the Missouri River. You may enjoy elk steaks, pork chops, grilled beef steaks, and some of the best fried chicken you ever tasted at the historic Arrow Rock Tavern, opened by Joseph Huston in 1834.

The tavern is available for banquets, wedding receptions, or other private gatherings, Wednesday through Sunday. It is a wonderful place to come for dinner before or after enjoying a play at the Lyceum Theatre in Arrow Rock.

While you are here, enjoy a tour of the old building and the mercantile store. You will think you are back in the 1830s!

Bon Appetit!
Glasgow, Mo.

June 10, A.D. 1804

Bon Appetit!

The Rolling Pin Bakery

Jeremy Sayler   *Tues.-Sat. 7:00-3:00*
Chef/Owner   *660-338-0800*

On Market Street, Glasgow, between First and Second Streets, the Rolling Pin Bakery is a fine lunch room that Georges Drouillard and other expedition members would have very much enjoyed.

Serving a variety of sandwiches on croissant rolls, and soups, and salads, with a selection of soft drinks including Dr. Pepper, this is much more than a bakery, having the ambience of a 19th Century store.

And what a bakery! Try a peach-and-blueberry pie, or muffins with coffee. Cake and cheesecake, turnovers and bagels, you can't go wrong when you patronize the Rolling Pin, or engaging them to cater a party!

Bon Appetit!

Bon Appetit!

Brunswick, Mo.,

Mouth of Grand River.
June 12-13, A.D. 1804

Bon Appetit!
Miami-Carrollton-Waverly, Mo.

(See Van Meter State Park, ancient homesite of the
Missouria Indian Tribe.)
14-17 June, A.D. 1804

Bon Appetít!
Lexington, Mo.

18-19 June, A.D. 1804

Bon Appetit!
Independence, Mo.

June 24, A.D. 1804

Bon Appetit!
North Kansas City, Mo.

June 25, A.D. 1804
Sept. 15, A.D. 1806

Bon Appetit!

Kansas City, Mo.

Mouth of Kanzas River
June 26-29, A.D. 1804
Sept. 15, A.D. 1806

Bon Appetít!
Weston, Mo.

(See Weston Bend State Park)
July 1, A.D. 1804
Sept. 14, 1806

Bon Appetit!
Rushville-St. Joseph, Mo.

(See Lewis and Clark State Park)
July 6-7, A.D. 1804
Sept. 12, A.D. 1806

Bon Appetit!
Rockport, Mo.

July 16, A.D. 1804
Sept. 11, A.D. 1806

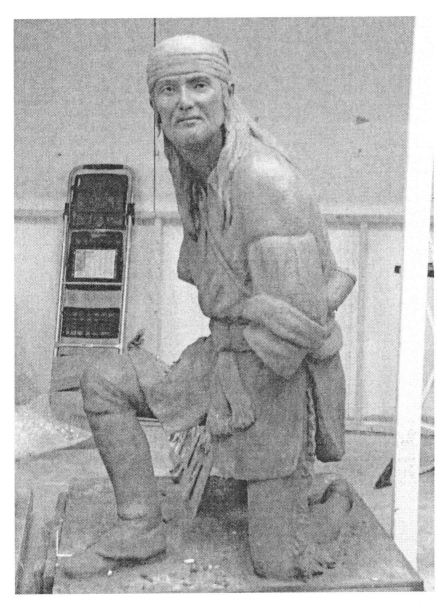

"Here's Looking at You!" Face-on view of unfinished model of statue of Georges P. Drouillard, by Sculptor Sabra Tull Meyer of Missouri.
(Photo at foundry by Jamie Meyer, 2006.)

Part II

The Life and Times of Georges P. Drouillard

Being a Compilation of what we have
Learned in Recent Historical Studies.

by

Historian Richard M. Gaffney, M.A.

A.D. 2006

Map I. Map showing western land claims of the 13 Colonies that became States, as of the Year 1783.
(By the author.)

Chapter I
Early Life and Education of Georges P. Drouillard

Georges Pierre Drouillard (using the French spelling) was the son of Capt. Pierre Drouillard, a French Canadian trader, scout, and interpreter, and a Shawnee woman whom he had taken as a wife. As a trader, it was "politic" for Pierre to have an Indian wife, and her presence helped him to learn the several Algonquian Indian languages and dialects of the tribes living in the lower Great Lakes area. It gave him *entrée* into the Indian villages of the region now called Ohio. On the manner of their marriage, we know nothing.

Baby Georges was born <u>about</u> A.D. 1770, date unknown, somewhere near Fort Detroit. [That was possibly the same year as T'kamthi (or Tecumtha, usually spelled Tecumseh), the well-known Shawnee war chief, was born.] At that time, Fort Detroit was in what the British government called Quebec. The territory included the area we now think of as the "old Northwest Territories" as well as what now is Ontario. It was claimed also by the Virginia Colony until after the American Revolution. Very definitely, it was the frontier.

Numerous books have been written about the Lewis and Clark Expedition, most of which at least mention Georges Drouillard. Some of the books' authors, looking at the man's name, refer to him as a "Frenchman," which neither he nor his father were. Some call him a "Canadian," which his father was, but Georges does not readily fall into such a characterization. Based on his choice of residence, as an adult, Georges should be called a Missourian. He made his home in what today is Cape Girardeau County.

His nationality truly was Shawnee, about which more is said, below.

One of the best documentaries about our subject is by M.O. Skarsten, of Forest Grove, Oregon, entitled, *George Drouillard, Hunter and Interpreter for Lewis and Clark, and Fur Trader, 1807-1810*, published in 1964 and reissued in 2003. His extensive bibliography gives significant credit to Walter B. Douglas, who provided editorial material and biographical sketches in the appendix of Thomas James' book, *Three Years Among the Indians and Mexicans*, published by the Missouri Historical Society in 1916. [James was a contemporary of Drouillard, engaged in the fur trade in the years following the return of the Lewis and Clark Expedition.]

His Value

The significance of the life of Georges Drouillard might best be found in a quotation from Mr. Skarsten's book (p. 18), a paragraph which captures the qualities of this man who is our subject:

> A cursory examination of the accomplishments of George Drouillard in behalf of the Lewis and Clark expedition will disclose that here lived a man of strong yet nimble physique, equally at home in the woods, on the plains, and in the mountains; a man of quick decision and vigorous action; enthusiastic, ardent, courageous, resourceful, likeable. It was the all-out competence of the man, his willingness—nay, even eagerness—to serve on any occasion, his unfailing reliability, his courage, tact, good judgement, and resourcefulness—it was qualities such as these that served, singly and in combination, to make him well-nigh indispensable in the furtherance of the project to which he

had committed himself. Of him can it truthfully be said: He ranked high among those energetic, gallant men whose claim to recognition lay in the fact that they served with honor and distinction the expedition commanded by Lewis and Clark; and, in so doing, the country to which they owed allegiance.

This was the view of an historian of the mid-20th Century, who found Drouillard one of the most valuable members of the expedition.

Indeed, the Lewis and Clark Trail Heritage Foundation, Inc., in *"The Eastern Legacy of Lewis and Clark,"* says of him, "Drouillard's services on the expedition place him second in importance to the captains."

And what did Captain Meriwether Lewis think of Drouillard?

> One of the two or three most valuable members of the expedition... a man of much merit; he has been peculiarly useful from his knowledge of the common language of gesticulation, and his uncommon skill as a hunter and woodsman. It was his fate also to have encountered on various occasions, with either Captain Clark or myself, all the most dangerous and trying scenes of the voyage, in which he uniformly acquitted himself with honor.

This is quoted by Author James Alexander Thom at the beginning of his historical novel, *Sign-Talker*, based on considerable research and his own knowledge of the Shawnee people. Thom's book is an insightful tale that goes far in explaining Georges Drouillard's conduct throughout his life.

Because Georges was such a capable member of the expedition, it is well that we of the 21st Century know more about this man who was called "Drewyer" in the *Journals* of Lewis and Clark. What is a great wonder to this author is that the man has been nearly ignored by so many who pretend to write histories or commentaries about the Voyage of Northwest Discovery and the adventures of the crew. In recent years, some "politically correct" commentators have done what they could to canonize Sacagawea and York, but still Drewyer has not been accorded the appreciation he deserves.

Skarsten, citing Douglas, notes that Pierre Drouillard married one Angelique Descamps in 1776. Young Georges might have been as old as six years by that time. Skarsten does not again mention Georges' Shawnee mother, but this does not mean that she had died or disappeared.

Alliances

The Declaration of Independence was published in that same year of 1776, assuring that there would be no retreat from the American War for Independence. The Shawnees had chosen to ally themselves with the French in the Seven Years' War (French and Indian War) and had helped demolish Gen. Braddock's British and Virginian Army in 1755, before they reached their destination of Fort DuQuesne (now Pittsburgh).

Following the French defeat in that war, Upper and Lower Canada had become known as Quebec under the British governance of the whole of eastern North America, 1763.

The British and the Iroquois League of Six Nations, meeting in 1763, in what now is Rome, New York, agreed to draw a line along the ridge of the Appalachian Mountains, with the land west of that line reserved to the Native People. The Proclamation Line of the Treaty of Fort Stanwix restricted the colonists of the Atlantic seaboard from settling west of the mountains. The Shawnee Nation then gave its alliance to the British in the American Revolutionary War. Obviously, it was their second wrong choice. The British were unable to enforce the treaty, to stem the surge of westward expansion, or to subdue the rebellious colonies. The result was Indian retaliations against the advance parties of settlers.

Stephen Warren, in his 2005 book, *The Shawnees and Their Neighbors, 1795-1870*, explains other alliances of the Shawnees, principally with the Delawares and the Kickapoos, but also with the Mingoes (mostly Seneca and Cayuga Iroquois), Wyandots, Ottawas, Potawatomies and others. Shawnees had intermarried with many other tribes, and therefore had kinship relations with many tribal bands, including even the Creeks of the Deep South, and Cherokees of the southern Appalachians.

Saying this, we must recognize that the Shawnees then entered a time of turmoil, as armies were formed and moved through the territory west of the Appalachians. We are not aware of the location of young Georges' residence at this time, but it is clear from his ability to sign his name that he must have had some schooling. His band of the Shawnee nation probably lived on the headwaters of the Maumee River in what now is northwestern Ohio (near Lima). A principal Shawnee location in that time would have been named Wapakoneta. Ottawa Indians lived in the Lower Maumee River Valley.

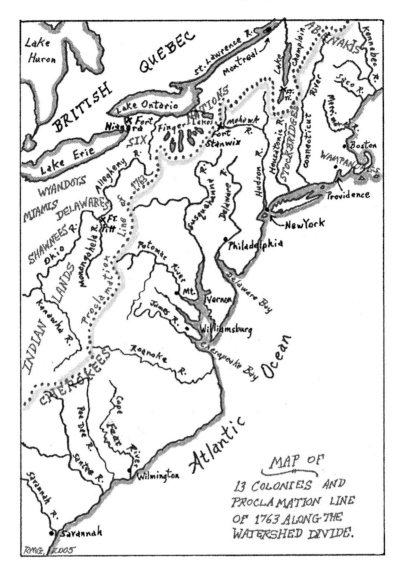

Map II. The territory of the 13 colonies, showing the Proclamation Line of 1763, drawn along the watershed of the Appalachian Mountain chain, and Indian Lands. (Major Indian nations shown, some on both sides of the line.)
(By the author.)

Bon Appetit!

Education

The boy Georges certainly was Christened in the Roman Catholic Church, and probably attended Roman Catholic mission schools off-and-on as a young child. Whether he was in a class of two or three, or a class of several we may never know. He may have achieved a third grade level of proficiency, probably in French language, and therefore he could read somewhat and write well enough to be able to sign his name. [More on that below.] The methods of instruction used in Catholic mission schools were very different from the methods used by Indian parents. This was especially true in regard to what we think of as discipline, and many can imagine nuns rapping knuckles with rulers. It is likely that Georges did not like his schooling. It is possible that he left his father's house and went to live with his Shawnee mother sometime in this period. Maybe his mother was never far away from Georges.

Evidently, Georges and his Shawnee mother were living among her people before the end of the Revolutionary War, which as we said was a time of considerable social disturbance among the Native tribes of the region west of the Appalachian Mountains. Georges' education during this period would have been of the traditional Algonquian type. An Indian boy's uncles would have been his teachers and disciplinarians. Young Georges would have been taught the skills and attitudes of his Shawnee uncles. The tribe lived in several bands in what now is called Ohio. Some of the bands lived close to the *Lenni Lenape* or Delaware people.

In 1782, American soldiers under the command of Gen. George Rogers Clark burned villages of the Shawnees (who favored the British in the war) and destroyed the trading post of Louis Lorimier, a Canadian trader married to Georges' Aunt Charlotte. [Skarsten wrote that perhaps Pierre Drouillard and Louis Lorimier were related, but it may have been only by marriage to two sisters or half-sisters.] Their villages and food supplies destroyed, the Shawnees were rendered destitute. Lorimier's trading post, with all his trade goods, also was gone, and he and his family were destitute. The hated Clark was nicknamed "Town Burner" by the Shawnees. [See Jones, *William Clark*, Ch. 2, esp. p. 45.]

The Shawnees took council to determine what to do. Naturally, there were two major factions that developed: One faction wanted to fight the bloody Americans to the death. One faction wanted to get away from the bloody Americans. There was a third option of trying to accommodate to the American invaders.

Several eastern Algonquian tribes were moving westward at this time, including the Delaware Indians (*Lenni Lenape*) who had been gradually moving westward for generations. Many of the Delawares had been converted to Christianity by Quakers or Moravian missionaries, and therefore were Protestants. [See Jones, *William Clark*, Ch. 2, esp. p. 43.] The Shawnees and Delawares are historically and linguistically close cousins. Quakers and Moravians sent missionaries among the various tribes in this time period.

Other nearby tribes or nations included the Wyandots (also called Hurons, an Iroquoian language people) and the Miamis (an Algonquian language people). Some of the Iroquoian tribes, also "punished" by American army expeditions during the Revolutionary War, splintered. Some Iroquois people who moved southwestward in this time period, mostly Seneca and Cayuga, became known as "Mingoes" (possibly from the Delaware name for the Iroquois, *Mengwe*). Most of the Iroquois were pagan, but many of the Mohawk Iroquois were Anglican Christians. Many religious partisans may have influenced young

Georges Drouillard at that time, including traditional Shawnee, Roman Catholic, and Protestant. This author believes that Georges was a Christian man in a Shawnee cultural setting.

Migration

Sometime after the Revolutionary War, the westward migration that had begun in the 1760s by white frontier folks from the Original Thirteen States, into what had been "Indian Country," picked up momentum. The Treaty of Fort Stanwix, 1763, was a British and Indian effort to keep American settlers out of Ohio, Kentucky, and other western lands. But with the end of the War for Independence, the Proclamation Line drawn by the Treaty of 1763 was no longer in effect. The "flood" of settlers into Shawnee lands was very disturbing to the Shawnees.

The name, "Shawnee," comes from the Delaware word, *Shawawno*, meaning "south" or "southerner." In the Indian oral traditions, hundreds of years earlier than this time, the *Shawanoes* separated from the Delawares, and went south. The French named them *Shawanaise*. The English colonists twisted not the Indian name, but the French name, into *Shawanese*. (This is similar to *Chinaise* in French becoming *Chinese* in English.) The settlers simply called them Shawnees. Because the Shawnee had, historically, been allies of the French and later the British, the American frontiersmen universally despised them. The feeling was mutual.

Warren, in his *The Shawnees and Their Neighbors, 1795-1870*, noted that there is a belief that other tribes noticed that the Shawnees lived near and associated with other southern tribes and called the Shawnees "southerners." The *Lenni Lenape* oral traditions and the name appear to be of an earlier origin.

Shawnee bands lived near and were friendly with the Cherokees of what now is western North Carolina for a period of their pre-historic time. Even later in history, the Cherokees, the Delawares, and the Shawnees were friendly toward each other. This is particularly notable during the late 1800s.

Large numbers of white settlers migrated into the Indian Country of Ohio, Kentucky, and Tennessee, and the Shawnees were particularly resentful of this intrusion into their lands. They were crowded by the American intruders, and greatly annoyed. Almost always, when American soldiers fought battles with the Indians, the Natives were outnumbered, outgunned, and outlasted. The Americans were land-hungry, or more to the point, land-greedy.

As we said, about 1782, young Georges Drouillard was living with his mother and her extended family in northwestern Ohio, probably in the Upper Maumee River Valley. Her brothers, his uncles, were surrogate fathers to the boy, in the absence of Pierre, providing instruction and discipline. They taught him Shawnee traditions. They took him hunting with them, teaching him first how to hunt with bow-and-arrow, and then with musket, powder, and ball. Young Georges learned well, and was blessed by the Great Maker with the skills of an adept hunter. Eventually, he matured into a Shawnee man.

A Shawnee Man

Although half French and half Shawnee, what the French call *metís*, Georges was accepted by the Shawnees as one of their own. The Shawnees had a long tradition of intermarrying with other tribes, and accepting those of other tribes into their own. (See Warren and Moorehead in the references.) He was taught how to be a Shawnee man, was taught Shawnee traditions, and was taught to be a responsible, dependable member of the tribe. Despite what some authors have claimed, he dressed, thought, and behaved like a Shawnee, not like a French Canadian man. In other words, culturally, Georges Drouillard was a Shawnee Indian man, *lenay*, and identified himself, socially, as part of the Shawnee nation. Those authors who write of him as a "Frenchman" do him and his people a disservice.

It is important to understand that the Shawnees were not then, and are not, now, a nation with a centralized government. Historically, there were five divisions of the Shawnees. The Maykujay (or Mekoche) Division, principally at Wapakoneta, Ohio, about 1800; the Chalagawtha Division [or Chillicothe]; the Piccaway (or Piqua) Division; the Kispokotha Division, and the Thawegila Division. Warren says that Tecumseh belonged to the Kispokotha Division. Moorehead, in *The Indian Tribes of Ohio,* p. 95, quoted Chief Black Hoof as saying that the Shawanoes had four tribes: Piqua, Mequachake, Kiskapocoke, and Chillicothe. Also, the several villages of the Shawnees were considered autonomous in their governance. By 1800, more than half of all people who considered themselves Shawnees were living in Upper Louisiana (Missouri).

What did Georges look like? He has been described as tall and straight. He surely was kept on a Shawnee cradle board, *t'kinagun,* as an infant, which has the effect of straightening the back for life. He almost certainly dressed as a Shawnee man (and there was much individuality in that). He probably wore a linen shirt and a linen hunting frock. But he most likely wore leather leggings and moccasins. He likely wore a hunting pouch over his shoulder, adorned with the trade silver ornaments typical of that time and place. He lived among the Shawnees (by choice) almost his entire life. What his face looked like is anyone's guess. Artists and sculptors really do not know.

Growth of the United States

Kentucky and Tennessee became States in the Union, along with Vermont (which did not want to be part of either New York or New Hampshire). Vermont became the 14th State, 1791; Kentucky became the 15th State, 1792, and the Congress established a new flag design, with fifteen stars and fifteen stripes, 1795. Known as the "Star Spangled Banner" in the National Anthem, it remained the official flag, even after Tennessee (the 16th) was added to the Union, 1796. Ohio (the 17th) was added in 1803. The Corps of Northwest Discovery, as it was called, carried the 15-star, 15-stripe flag with them.

Portrait of Chief Kishkalwa, about 1825. He moved his people from what now is Ohio across what now are Indiana and Illinois, and across the Mississippi River into what now is Missouri, during the years 1782-1797. This portrait by artist Charles Bird King probably was painted during the chief's visit to Washington, D.C., in 1825, some 40 years after leading his people away from the "bloody Americans."
(Source: Moore, Robert, NATIVE AMERICANS, 1997.)

Chapter 2

Chief Kishkalwa and Moving to Missouri

In this time period, 1782 and after (Georges was about age 12 in 1782), many Shawnees began looking for a new home, and went westward, hoping to find respite from war. Chief Kishkalwa's band of Shawnees (which probably included Georges and his mother) migrated westward over several years across what now are Indiana and southern Illinois.

During this same time period, Louis Lorimier, his wife, Charlotte, and their several children moved across the Mississippi River into Spanish Louisiana. The Spanish welcomed Catholic settlers, and the oath of allegiance was dual in nature: To the Spanish crown and to the Roman church.

Louis Lorimier and family settled first in the Sainte Genevieve District of Upper Louisiana, the earliest French-speaking settlement in the Territory. The earliest French settlement west of the Mississippi was near their river bottom farmlands, known to them as *les grand champs*. After the Great Flood of 1785, the settlers moved their residences up onto the hilly land above the flood plains of the Mississippi, where Ste. Genevieve now stands.

According to Historian Louis Houck, in the first volume of his *A History of Missouri*, page 208, Shawnee and Delaware Indians were being allowed to come into Spanish Louisiana Territory (sometimes called Spanish Illinois) as early as 1784, "not only to protect the [earlier French] settlements against the Osage Indians, but also to strengthen the west bank of the Mississippi against the Americans." But we know that the Indians were moving *away from* the Americans.

Historian William E. Foley, in his *The Genesis of Missouri*, wrote, p. 64, that "by 1787 a reported twelve hundred Shawnees and six hundred Delawares accepted the Tory trader's [Lorimier's] invitation and settled along the Saline, Apple, Cinque Hommes, and Flora creeks south of Ste. Genevieve."

Warren says that Methoataske, the mother of Tecumseh, moved to Upper Louisiana as early as 1779. She was a Creek by birth, married to a Shawnee, and widowed. She was in the vanguard of those Shawnees who went westward, looking for a safe haven in which the Shawnees could live.

Prospering in his business and in his relations with the Spanish government (most of the members of which were of French descent), Louis Lorimier was able to secure a grant of land south of Sainte Genevieve. Foley wrote, p. 65, that "sometime around 1792, Lorimier moved from Saline Creek to Cape Girardeau."

He picked a location along a bend in the river called Cape Girardeau (formerly spelled Girardot), just above the mouth of the Ohio River. He established a new trading post and encouraged settlement in the area. The Spanish government made him the commandant of the new territorial district, called him "Don Luis Lorimier," and allowed him to offer land grants to the tribes, for settlement.

What tribes? Apparently more than just the Shawnees and Delawares. Foley wrote, page 65, "A 1797 report indicated the presence of Shawnee, Delaware, Peoria, Illinois, Miami, Ottawa, Mascouten, Kickapoo, and Potawatomi Indian camps in Spanish Illinois."

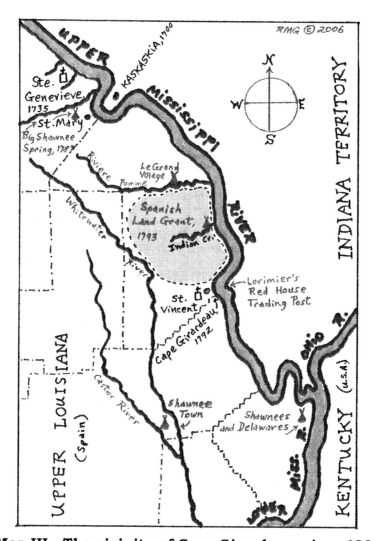

Map III. The vicinity of Cape Girardeau, circa 1800, showing Shawnee settlements. (Modern county lines added in Missouri to assist the reader. Map by the author, 2006, not drawn to scale; width of rivers exaggerated purposely, courses approximate. Area of Spanish land grant to the Shawnees is only approximate, as are locations of Shawnee villages.)
Sources include Denny and Harlan, Atlas of Lewis and Clark in Missouri; Warren, The Shawnees and their Neighbors, Jackson, "Cape Girardeau and the Corps of Discovery," and other writings.

Lorimier's old friends, the Shawnees of Chief Kishkalwa's band, including his wife's sister and her sister's son, Georges Drouillard, surely were among those he encouraged to move across to the Louisiana Territory. Houck, p. 212, wrote that among the Shawnees of Apple Creek lived one Peter Cornstalk (son of the Chief Cornstalk who was prominent during the Revolutionary War), and that "another chief was Kiscalawa (tiger tail)."

Warren, in his 2005 book, wrote that Kishkalwa lived among the Creeks in Alabama until 1785 (page 74). We are unsure of this. Might there have been more than one Shawnee named Kishkalwa? Or might this one chief have had kinfolk living among the Creeks, and he visited them and then returned to Ohio and later moved to Louisiana Territory? Warren does not write any more about Kishkalwa, and this author continues to search for more information. History has many riddles.

These Shawnees were welcomed by the Spanish government of the Louisiana Territory, and settled in that part of Upper Louisiana that became known as Cape Girardeau County, Missouri. [Chief Kishkalwa's portrait was one of many portraits of prominent Native leaders made from life by artist Charles Bird King. The occasion of the portrait-painting was the chief's visit to Washington, D.C., as part of a treaty making, 1825.)

The Spanish land grant, dated 1793, was for land located eastward of Whitewater River, westward of the Mississippi River, and south of Apple River. *Le grand village des Shawanaise* was situated north of Apple River. [See map.]

Many Shawnees settled along the Apple River, planting apple orchards and vegetable gardens. They hunted in the forest for their meat. Their settlement numbered about 400 souls, and was one of the largest settlements in Upper

Bon Appetit!

APPLE CREEK SHAWNEE, BY WARIN.—FROM COLLOT'S DANS L'AMERIQUE

Depiction of a Shawnee man of the Apple Creek settlement in Upper Louisiana, as contained in Houck's A History of Missouri, 1908, citing the artist and the source.

Louisiana. [St. Louis and Ste. Genevieve each had about 1,000. St. Charles had about 450. The Apple River Shawnee band would have been the fourth largest settlement in Upper Louisiana, but Indians didn't count.] The region still produces fruit crops. The nearest modern town is Appleton, and the stream is called Apple Creek, today.

Historian Houck includes a drawing of an Apple River Shawnee man in his book, but does not explain the artist or the date of the drawing (which see). The drawing shows a man wearing tightly fitting leggings with side flaps that appear fringed, and garters below the knee. He wears moccasins with side flaps. He appears to be wearing an overshirt with one armband showing, the presumed other armband covered by a mantle ("matchcore") or blanket. The loincloth is short. A waist belt or sash cannot be seen, but the lower edge of the shirt appears gathered as if by a belt or sash, which would be a logical item of garb. The man is equipped with a bow and arrows, but no quiver is shown. There is a strap across one shoulder, and again we presume it is for a hunting pouch. The man's ears appear to be larger than normal, perhaps to allow the artist to call attention to the ears' ornaments under short hair. He may be wearing a "choker" necklace of some sort. If the time period represented by this image is the late 18th Century, then Georges Drouillard might have dressed in the manner shown, at least while he was at home in the Cape Girardeau District.

James Denny and James Harlan, in their *Atlas* (please refer to the list of references), wrote of the Shawnee village seven miles up Apple River as the largest of the Absentee Shawnee villages. Knowing that President Jefferson wanted the American Indians to take up farming and become integrated into (white) American agricultural society, Denny and Harlan wrote that these Shawnees "were Jefferson's kind of Indians." They lived in permanent homes, fenced their farms, and maintained good relations with their neighbors.

We presume that Georges visited Uncle Louis' trading post often, trading deerskins ("bucks") for trade goods. There were other Shawnee and Delaware settlers living near Indian Creek, and also south of Lorimier's "Red House" trading post, in what now is the Bird's Point area of Mississippi County, Missouri.

It was while trading and helping at the post that young Georges would have learned more arithmetic, learned Spanish and English languages, and encountered other Indians of many tribes, including Great Plains tribes of farther west, who spoke using sign language. It appears that Georges had a facility for learning languages, for he became known for his ability in translating among the various Algonquian Indian languages, French, Spanish, and English, and in talking with signs.

It is certain that Georges was a hunter and trapper in what now is southern Missouri, including the Ozarks and the flat flood plains south of the rocky outcroppings known as Cape Girardeau and Crowley's Ridge. He took his catches home, where some was used within the family, and some was taken to the trading post for sale on the economy. In this way, Georges became a self-supporting, productive member of Shawnee society.

On His Own

About 1800, 30-year-old Georges Drouillard's mother "walked the Spirit Trail to the Happy Hunting Ground." After this, he went off on his own, becoming a meat hunter for the U.S. Army post at Fort Massac, Indiana Territory (now Illinois), on the lower Ohio River. It was at Fort

The Signing of the Treaty. This sculpture was designed by Karl Bitter for the 1904 World's Fair in St. Louis, known as the Louisiana Purchase Centennial Exposition. After the Fair, it was brought to Jefferson City for permanent display. It depicts Robert Livingston, standing, left, and James Monroe, seated, for the United States, and François Barbé-Marbois, signing, for France, 1803. By the treaty, the U.S.A. acquired Louisiana Territory from France for $15,000,000. The Treaty sculpture faces the north front of the Missouri State Capitol.
(Photo by the author, 2006.)

Massac in November, 1803, that Georges met Captains Lewis and Clark (and Clark's manservant, York). They invited him to join them in their Voyage of Discovery up the Missouri River, with an intention to cross over to the Pacific Ocean. Capt. Daniel Bissell, post commandant, recommended Georges to Lewis and Clark. They needed a good hunter and an interpreter. Georges was the kind of man they needed.

As would have been a Shawnee man's custom, Georges gave the matter considerable thought and prayer, and worked as a courier for Captains Lewis and Clark for about a month and a half before deciding that he would sign on for the expedition. Why did he go? Possibly it was curiosity, that he wanted to learn more, see what was up the river, see what was over the mountains, or see the Pacific Ocean. Or it may have been his intention to find a location for a trading post of his own. We cannot know with certainty, but he may have been like the bear that went over the mountain: "To see what he could see."

The Louisiana Purchase

President Thomas Jefferson sent a diplomatic mission to France to inquire if the U.S. might purchase the port of New Orleans from the French (who recently had secretly re-acquired Louisiana from Spain). New Orleans was then, as now, a major seaport for the export of American farm products, and the Mississippi River was a major highway for the transport of farm products of western states. Napoleon, recognizing his inability to hold onto Louisiana while battling the British in Europe, and in need of cash, decided to offer all of the territory to the U.S.

There is a sculpture facing the north front of the Missouri Capitol Building that commemorates the signing of the Louisiana Purchase Treaty. Shown are Robert Livingston, James Monroe, and Barbé-Marbois of France. This is the only sculpture known to depict the treaty-signing.

Following the ratification of the U.S. purchase of Louisiana from Emperor Napoleon of France, in March, 1804, the Spanish flag came down at St. Louis. The French tricolor went up for 24 hours. Then the French flag came down, and the national flag of the United States went up. The Shawnees who thought they had gotten away from the "bloody Americans" by moving to Spanish Louisiana found themselves residing in the U.S. Louisiana Territory. That must have come as a shock to that tribe of refugees! (Can you imagine?)

Georges went on the journey as a civilian employee, not a soldier. He was hired (at $25 per month, as opposed to the $5 per month earned by the soldiers of the expedition) to provide service as an interpreter among the Indian tribes they would meet on the trip, and to hunt for meat to feed the men of the Corps of Northwest Discovery. He did his job well, so well in fact that Lewis and Clark awarded him double for his services when they returned to St. Louis, and gave him high praise, especially for his dependability.

Chapter 3
Study of Drouillard's Signature

In 1804, as the Corps of Discovery passed up the Missouri River, the captains stopped frequently, and climbed high bluffs to look around and take their bearings. East of Jefferson City, they went up what today is called "Clark's Hill," June 2, 1804, and measured longitude and latitude at the mouth of the Osage River.

Passing up the Missouri, upriver from the site of the City of Jefferson and the State Capitol Building, the next prominent feature they explored was what today is called Sugar Loaf Rock, June 4, 1804. Historian James M. Denny, in his book, *Lewis and Clark in the Manitou Bluffs Region*, a revision of his earlier work, *Lewis and Clark in the Boonslick*, provides a marvelous description of Sugar Loaf Rock and the certainty of its identification, based on Captain Clark's descriptions.

A third prominent rock outcropping at the river's edge, today called Bull Rock, is a small eminence, not nearly as striking in appearance as Sugar Loaf Rock. Probably on June 5, 1804, Captain Clark and others examined this rock, also, as it may have had engravings on the river side called "Manitous."

The Manitous

Manitou is an Algonquian Indian word that means "maker." The term, *Gitchee Manitou*, in turn, means "Great Maker," the Algonquian name for the King of the Universe, Almighty God, *El Shaddai*, the Creator of all things. In the Algonquian understanding, the Great Maker made lesser makers to help with the task of Creation. The term is preserved in its French spelling in the name of Moniteau County and Moniteau Creek, west of Jefferson City.

Enhanced image of the signature of "G.P. DrouiLLard's" presumably made in 1804 on the soft limestone or dolomite of Bull Rock, a bluff face on the right bank of the Missouri River upstream of Jefferson City, Mo.
(Image courtesy of Mr. Quentin Wade, Cole County, Mo.)

The Sauk (or Sac), "People of the Yellow Earth," and Fox (or Mesquaki), "People of the Red Earth," Indians were then and are today tribes that are cousins to each other and speak close dialects of the Algonquian language family, like Kickapoo, Potawatomi, and others. The Sauks and Foxes were then frequent visitors to the Missouri River Valley, using the river as a highway to hunting grounds farther west. They used the pale grey colored dolomite cliffs and bluffs of the Missouri River as "billboards" to record the locations of good springs of fresh water (very helpful on a muddy river), or salt springs ("licks"), and to propitiate the Manitous who resided in the region.

Spoken of today by historians as the Little Manitou Bluffs Region, as distinguished from the greater Manitou Bluffs Region farther upriver (near Rocheport), these outcroppings of rock were noticed by travelers who passed by water. In his book, Jim Denny gives excellent comments on these locations. Georges Drouillard certainly was familiar with the religious connotations of the engravings, which were painted with red ochre (mixed with grease, making a durable grease paint), or sometimes inlaid with darker colored stones.

The Bull Rock Inscriptions

The expedition paused, possibly on June 4 or 5, 1804, to explore the area around "Bull Rock." They may have left their initials, scratched into the soft stone, as a record of their visit. Nearly a century later, as work crews were building a railroad line along the south bank of the Missouri River, a photographer took a picture of the landward rock face of Bull Rock where a number of figures, names and initials had been carved "in the old days." Date of photo: Uncertain, perhaps 1901.

The bases of Bull Rock and other outcroppings in the valley have been scrubbed smooth by several major floods since the turn of the last century, most notably by the floods of 1903, 1951-52 and 1993-95. Any initials once scratched in the rock are gone, today. But the photographs survive.

Mr. Quentin Wade of Cole County, Mo., in examining one century-old photograph in 2005, discovered hand-inscribed names and initials, and various animal figures he presumes to have been made by Indians. Mr. Wade enlarged and enhanced the photograph in order to make out the inscriptions. He discovered an "M.L." and a "W.C.", plus Georges Drouillard's "signature," with double capital Ls. [See illustration.] Proof that Georges could write? Or at least sign his name? Read on.

A signature also appears on a promissory note for $301.63 and 1/3, dated at Fort Massac, February 11, 1804. (That would be just a few months earlier than the inscription on Bull Rock.) The signature appears to this author to be in the hand of whoever wrote the note, and

Historian Richard M. Gaffney, M.A.

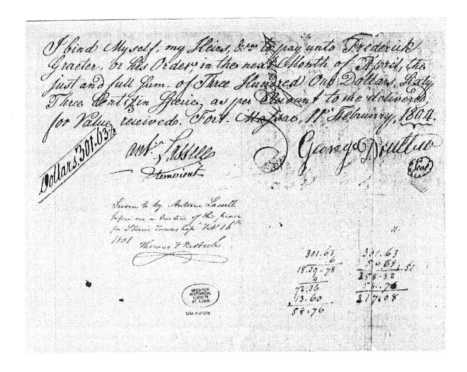

Copy of a Promissory Note for $301.63 and 1/3 from Georges Drouillard to Frederick Graeter, dated 11 February, 1804, at Fort Massac, showing his signature. The witness's name is Antoine Lasselle.
(From the Manuel Lisa Papers, courtesy of the Missouri Historical Society, St. Louis, Mo., Rocheport),

the name is not spelled correctly. It is, however, regarded as authentic by most historians. The original is in the Manuel Lisa Papers of the Missouri Historical Society, St. Louis. [See illustration.]

There are other examples, with later dates, as we shall see.

After returning from the Pacific Coast, Georges Drouillard resumed his residence in the Cape Girardeau District (County, in the state nomenclature), Territory of Upper Louisiana, later to become the State of Missouri. St. Louis was the eastern terminus of the fur trade of the day, the principal fur trade entrepreneurs being the Chouteau Family (French) and Manuel Lisa (Spanish).

It is apparent that Georges traveled often to and from St. Louis on business, because he subsequently joined Manuel Lisa on two fur trapping-trading expeditions into the Upper Missouri River Valley.

A promissory note document from the Bates Family Papers in the Missouri Historical Society reads in part as follows:

> "...Alexander McNeir their heirs and assigns, forever._____
> In testimony whereof the said George Dreuillard hath hereunto subscribed his name and affixed his seal, at the town of St. Louis aforesaid, the day and year first above written.___
> Signed sealed and delivered
> In presence of_____   Geo Druillur (Seal)
>
>   John Connor (S)
>   Lawrence Gibbon   (S)
>
> Territory of Louisiana
> District of St. Louis_____
> Before me the subscriber one of the Justices of the court of Common pleas in & for the district aforesaid Personally came this day the above named George Druiliard, who acknowledged the above, on [indistinct] of writing to be

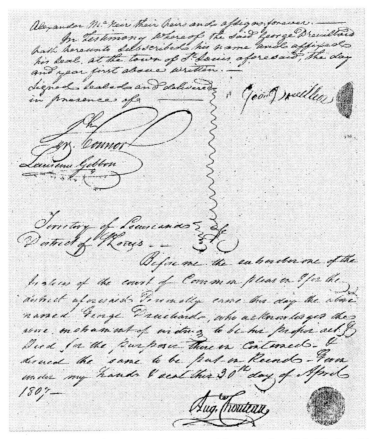

Copy of Promissory Note to Alexander McNeir, 30 April, 1807.
(From the Bates Family Papers, courtesy of the Missouri Historical Society, St. Louis, Mo.)

his proper act., & Deed for the purpose therein Contained & desired the same to be put on Record__ Given under my hand & seal this 30th day of April
1807__   Aug.te Chouteau   [Seal]

[See illustration.]

Nearly two years later, following Drouillard's second journey up the Missouri River to its sources, another document bore his signature. From the Fur Trade Collection at the Missouri Historical Society, it reads as follows:

> Bellefontaine March 25 1809
>
> For value Received I promise
> Joseph Kimball on his order Nineteen
> dollars payable at six months
> after Date.   George Drullard (S)
>
> Witness
> Chs. Williams (S)
>
> *Pour* [indistinct] [indistinct] *le 27ʰ Jan. 1812_* [indistinct] *anne et* [indistinct]
>   2.66.
>   [indistinct] *en Billet*   . . . 19.
> $ 21.66.

[See illustration.] Note that Georges Drouillard was dead by Jan. 27, 1812.

Another document from 1809, between his two post-expedition journeys to the Upper Missouri River, from the Manuel Lisa Papers at the Missouri Historical Society, is a page from a legal deposition given by Georges Drouillard. It reads as follows:

> "...thing, except as you have stated above, and of the charging me for $162 which he said had been taken by me:
> Answer: I do not personally know of your taking any thing more: Mr. Manuel & Benito Vasquez took an Inventory and found as Mr. Manuel and Benito told me $162, missing—
>
> Question by Defense Attorney
> Did Etienne after that desert from Mr. Manuel?

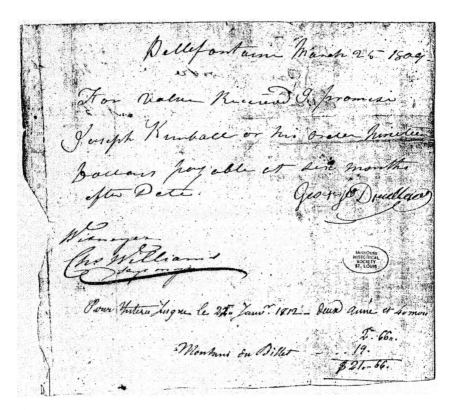

Copy of a Promissory Note for $19 from Georges Drouillard to Joseph Kimball, dated 25 March, 1809, at Bellefontaine, Mo.
(From the Fur Trade Collection, courtesy of the Missouri Historical Society, St. Louis, Mo.)

Bon Appetit!

Ans.　　Yes_____ He deserted & went among
the Indians [brought(?)] back a horse which he
sold for $50__ and when Etienne started from St.
Louis, on the voyage, he had nothing.
Q. by Plaintiff—Did you keep Mr. Manuel's books?
Answer –No—
Q. by Same—Did you ever examine the Books
to see how much Brant (?) had charged him
[indistinct] with?
Answer—I did not---
Q. by Same—Were you concerned in the
[indistinct] with Manuel?
Answer—I was—
Q. by Same—Do you know of Mr. Manuel having
[indistinct] any other person to go in the store &
deal out goods?
Answer—None but himself, Etienne Brant, Mayett
& myself—
Q. by Same—Do you know of defendant having
pointed a gun at Plaintiff and threatened to shoot
him—
Answer-- I do not—　　George Druillard (S)
Sworn to and subscribed before Me
The 26th day of April 1809

[indistinct] J.P. (S.)

(See illustration.)

A comparison of these signatures shows us that he commonly wrote his own Christian name in the English form (without a silent final s, which would be the French spelling). Also, he did not seem to use a standard spelling for his surname, it appearing as Drullard, Druillar, Drulliur, and variations, with the silent, final d subservient to the other letters in the signature.

In addition, the slant of the letters shows that he was right-handed, and had been taught penmanship to some degree. But in a time when many residents of the frontier knew only enough of writing to sign their own names,

Historian Richard M. Gaffney, M.A.

Copy of an excerpt from a faded original of a legal deposition given by Georges Drouillard, dated 26 April, 1809, in St. Louis, showing Drouillard's signature. Note the old-style "long-tailed s" used in the script on this document.
(From the Manuel Lisa Papers, courtesy of the Missouri Historical Society, St. Louis, Mo.)

and otherwise were functionally illiterate, individuals' signatures were apt to vary through time.

Signatures have always been very important to American Indians. Before learning to use handwriting (cursive script), American Indians used pictographs to represent themselves on letters or other documents, such as treaties or maps. While it is clear that all individuals' signatures vary somewhat, there usually is an attempt to keep them consistent. Georges' capital G and capital D are the most consistent letters in his signatures.

Obviously, Georges Drouillard was not a college graduate. How much actual classroom schooling he had is conjectural. How much help he was to Uncle Louis Lorimier, or to Manual Lisa, or to the Captains on the Lewis and Clark Trail, in matters of written documents has not been recorded. The *Drewyer Journals* of the expedition, if any, have not been found. So what do we make of this?

This author suspects that there are pay receipts and other records which will be researched and other signatures of Georges Drouillard will be located in the future. Further comparisons may bring us to additional conclusions about his ability to write and the nature of his personal signature. In the meantime, this is a chance for all of us to speculate, but it appears that the signatures shown are authentic.

The signature inscription on the back face of Bull Rock, scratched into soft dolomite with the sharp point of a knife blade (perhaps), more than two hundred years ago, was photographed at a time when hardly anyone had ever heard of Georges Drouillard, in a location then nearly inaccessible. We therefore have no reason to suspect a forgery. Nevertheless, that signature looks different from the others. History has many riddles.

Chapter 4
How "Drewyer" Is Being Remembered

While on the expedition, Georges, as a civilian, did not stand sentry duty, and did not eat with the soldiers. He was part of the "Captains' mess." Each of the three sergeants, in charge of a platoon, had a "mess," also. And, in the first part of the voyage, the *engagés* (hired men) had their own dining arrangements.

In the first part of the journey, Drouillard, sometimes a solitary hunter, often slept away from the flotilla of boats, as he ranged some distance from the river for game. He probably had his own piece of canvas to rig at night to keep off the dew or rain, and many nights he was absent from the rest of the crew.

After leaving Fort Mandan, where Drouillard had "bachelor quarters," the boats carried Sacagawea's tepee. Was the tepee just for Sacagawea and her husband and child? Actually, they <u>and</u> the two captains <u>and</u> Drewyer were regular occupants of that lodge. Probably York and Seaman slept under the stars when the weather was benign, but during inclement weather, they also slept in the tepee. That probably was very tight quarters, as most skin tepees in those days were not large, and this one was rigged with oars and push-poles from the boats.

Of course, Drouillard pitched in with the work, but much of the time, he was either hunting or butchering; skinning or flensing; or even tanning skins to make leather. We can be sure his hands were seldom idle. So it was appropriate that he was not occupied as the soldiers were, and, as the chief interpreter (and a civilian) that he was accorded a place with the officers of the Corps.

Photo of a Maquette of the Lewis and Clark Bicentennial Capitol Monument by sculptor Sabra Tull Meyer, 2006, showing the Corps of Discovery figures (l-r) of York, Capt. Lewis, Seaman, Capt. Clark, and Georges Drouillard.
(Photo by Col. John Tandy.)

Later, Georges, then an experienced explorer of the Upper Missouri River, became a partner with Manuel Lisa, a Spanish fur trader of St. Louis, and went back up the Missouri, trapping for furs. Between journeys, he resided in what now is Cape Girardeau County, Missouri. We have learned that he raised horses at his home, there. Jane Randol Jackson of Cape Girardeau, researching the Estate Papers of Louis Lorimier in the county records, found information on Georges Drouillard. His probate court papers are in St. Louis, and Louis Lorimier was an executor of Georges' estate.

On his final trip up the Missouri, in 1810, it was reported that Georges was killed by Blackfoot Indians, *Piegan*, near the Three Forks of the Missouri, in what now is Montana. (See Holmberg, "A Man of Much Merit," p. 12.)

In 2003, the Shawnee Nation (Oklahoma) issued a bicentennial commemorative silver dollar in honor of the late Georges Drouillard.

And in 2006-7, the City of Jefferson Lewis and Clark Bicentennial Task Force, working in conjunction with the State of Missouri, city government, the National Park Service, and numerous private donors, facilitated the design and construction of a bronze Capitol Monument cluster located on grounds of the State Capitol Complex adjacent to the Jefferson Landing State Historic Site.

Bearing five heroic size figures that commemorate the Journey of the Corps of Discovery through Missouri, one of the figures is that of Georges Drouillard, the Missourian. This figure is the only statue of Georges of which we are aware. In the monument, he represents Missourians who participated in the journey. There were several from St. Charles, as well as "Drewyer." In addition, he represents those of Native American stock in the way that the figure of York represents those of African ancestry who made up the diverse crew of the Corps of Northwest Discovery.

We all can be proud of the accomplishments of those who went on the epic voyage of discovery, 1803 – 1806. They were as truly "on their own" after leaving "the east coast of Missouri," as the astronauts were, after leaving "the east coast of Florida," on their way to the moon. The greatest difference: The astronauts were able to communicate to "Mission Control," in Houston, and the crew of the Discovery Expedition were *incommunicado.*

Georges Drouillard should be remembered for the qualities that he brought to the challenges he faced. He was an honorable man who was trustworthy, loyal, helpful, and so on. To our knowledge, the saddest action that "Drewyer" would relate to us, if he could, took place in 1808, when he was dispatched to find and return a deserter from the Lisa Expedition up the Missouri River. Lisa's orders were to bring him back, "dead or alive." Probably in self-defense, Georges wounded the deserter. Subsequently, the deserter died. Some time later, accused of murder in that case, Drewyer was tried and found not guilty of the charge. (Murder, by definition, is pre-meditated.) In most of Drouillard's personal history, his character and his reputation were the same: He had integrity. He was an exemplar of what we can aspire to be.

The thought occurs that perhaps he will no longer be ignored by historians or the People of the State of Missouri, who should be proud of him.

-12 June, 2006.

Shawnee Hunter and Interpreter Georges P. Drouillard, as portrayed by Historian Richard M. Gaffney, during the 2004 re-enactment of the start of the expedition from Camp DuBois, Mississippi River. The Missouri shoreline is in the distance. Crew members of the Discovery Expedition of St. Charles are shown.
(Photo by Gerald D. Manchester.)

Suggested Reading/More Sources of Information

Ambrose, Stephen, *Undaunted Courage*, a biography of Meriwether Lewis (mentions Drouillard), New York: 1996.

Carter, Clarence Edwin, Compiler and Editor, *The Territorial Papers of the United States*, volumes regarding the Territory of Louisiana-Missouri, 1815-1821, Washington, D.C.: U.S. Government Printing Office, 1951.

Circle of Tribal Advisors, National Council of the Lewis & Clark Bicentennial, *A Guide to Visiting the Lands of Many Nations*, 2004. (Lists Shawnee bands, Ohio and Oklahoma.)

Denny, James M., *Lewis and Clark in the Boonslick*, Boonslick Historical Society, Boonville, Mo., 2000. (Lower Missouri River region.)

Denny, James M., and Harlan, James, *Atlas of Lewis and Clark in Missouri*, Columbia, Mo.: University of Missouri Press, 2003.

Dufur, Brett, *Lewis and Clark's Journey across Missouri*, Fayette, Mo.: A special publication of *Missouri Life* magazine, 2003.

Duncan, Dayton, and Burns, Ken, *LEWIS & CLARK, The Journey of the Corps of Discovery, an illustrated history* (mentions Drouillard), New York: Alfred A. Knopf, 1997.

Foley, William E., *Wilderness Journey, The Life of William Clark*, Columbia, Mo., University of Missouri Press, 2004.

Foley, William E., *The Genesis of Missouri: From Wilderness Outpost to Statehood*, Columbia, Mo.: University of Missouri Press, 1989.

Gilman, Carolyn, *Lewis and Clark across the Divide*, Washington, D.C.: Smithsonian Books, in association with the Missouri Historical Society, 2003.

Hammond's American History Atlas, C.S. Hammond & Co., Maplewood, N.J.: 1959.

Hétu, Richard, *The Lost Guide*, [historical novel about Toussaint Charbonneau] (mentions Drouillard), New York: East Village Press, 2004.

Holmberg, James J., "A Man of Much Merit," in *We Proceeded On*, Vol. 26, No. 3, August, 2000, pp. 8 ff., published by The Lewis and Clark Trail Heritage Foundation (mostly tells about Drouillard's post-expedition career and death), Great Falls, Montana.

Houck, Louis, *A History of Missouri, from the Earliest Explorations and Settlements until the Admission of the State into the Union*, Chicago, Ill.: R.R. Donnelley and Sons, 1908.

Jackson, Jane Randol, "Cape Girardeau and the Corps of Discovery," in *We Proceeded On*, Vol. 31, No. 1, February, 2005, pp. 14 ff., published by The Lewis and Clark Trail Heritage Foundation (mentions Drouillard and other members of the Corps of Discovery, after the conclusion of the expedition), Great Falls, Montana.

Jones, Landon Y., *William Clark and the Shaping of the West*, New York: Hill and Wang, a division of Farrar, Straus and Giroux, 2004.

Kagan, Hilde Heun, Ed., *The American Heritage Pictorial Atlas of United States History*, New York: 1966.

Lee, Patrick, *Mosquitoes, Gnats & Prickly Pear Cactus: The Lewis and Clark Review* (abridged Journals, mentions Drouillard), Jefferson Books, Ashland, Mo., 2005.

MacGregor, Carol Lynn, Ed., *Journals of Sgt. Patrick Gass*, Missoula, Mont., Mountain Press, 1997. (Gass did not ever use Drewyer's name in his journal, speaking only of "the hunters," an interesting fact that may reveal an attitude.)

McMullin, Phillip W., Editor, *Grassroots of America: A Computerized Index to the American State Papers, Land Grants and Claims, 1789-1837,* © 1972; Republished by the Southern Historical Press, © 1990.

Moore, Robert J., Jr., *NATIVE AMERICANS, A Portrait: The Art and Travels of Charles Bird King, George Catlin, and Karl Bodmer*, New York: Stewart, Tabori & Chang, 1997. (Source of Charles Bird King's portrait of Chief Kishkalwa of the Shawnees, and other portraits of early 19th Century Shawnees.)

Moore, Robert J., Jr., and Haynes, Michael, *Lewis and Clark, Tailor Made, Trail Worn*, Helena, Mont.: Farcountry Press, 2003. (Contains illustrations of what Drouillard might have worn on the expedition).

Moorehead, Warren King, *The Indian Tribes of Ohio*, Waterville, Ohio: Smoke & Fire Company, undated (purchased in 2006) no ©; being reprinted from The Ohio Archeological and Historical Publications, Volume VII, 1899.

Nute, Grace Lee, *The Voyageur*, St. Paul, Minn.: Minnesota Historical Society, 1955. (Gives insight into French Canadian *voyageurs* of Lower Canada.)

Oglesby, Richard Edward, *Manuel Lisa and the Opening of the Missouri Fur Trade*, Norman, Okla., University of Oklahoma Press, © 1963.

Rogers, Ann, *Lewis and Clark in Missouri*, Columbia, Mo.: University of Missouri Press, 3rd Edition, 2002. (Mentions Drouillard many times.)

Ronda, James P., *Lewis & Clark among the Indians*, Lincoln, Nebr., Univ. of Nebraska Press, 1984. (Mentions Drouillard.)

Skarsten, M.O., *George Drouillard, Hunter and Interpreter for Lewis and Clark and Fur Trader, 1807-1810*, Glendale, California, the Arthur H. Clark Company, 1964. (Contains much good primary information, including documents from the Missouri Historical Society, St. Louis.)

Slaughter, Thomas P., *Exploring Lewis and Clark*, New York: Alfred A. Knopf, 2003. (Mentions Drouillard.)

Thom, James Alexander, *Sign Talker*, New York, Ballantine Books, 2000. (Fictional account of the Adventure of George Drouillard on the Expedition, based on numerous facts and the author's extensive knowledge of the Shawnee People. Highly recommended historical novel for adult readers.)

Thrapp, Dan L., *Encyclopedia of Frontier Biography*, Lincoln, Nebr.: University of Nebraska Press, © 1988.

Warren, Stephen, *The Shawnees and Their Neighbors, 1795-1870*, Urbana, Ill.: University of Illinois Press, © 2005. (Anthropological historical review with strong sociological explanations of kinship ties and multiethnic alliances; valuable chiefly for explaining the decentralized nature of Shawnee village life and governance; based in part on interviews with living Shawnees who were able to convey their oral histories and traditional cultural patterns.)

Shawnee Hunter and Interpreter Georges P. Drouillard in Hunting Camp with flintlock short rifle, pack basket, canoe paddle, and shelter tarp as portrayed by Historian R.M. Gaffney.
(Color photo by Dolores White Dove Gaffney, Cherokee.)

Part III

Bon Appetít!

and

The Life and Times of Georges P. Drouillard

by

Historian Richard M. Gaffney. M.A.

Acknowledgements

Special thanks to Mr. Allen Schroll of Turkey Foot Trading Company and Forge, LLC, of Madison, Missouri, for introducing me to Chief Kishkalwa of the Shawnees. He was the first one ever to mention the name of that important subchief of the Shawnees, as I was researching the life and times of Georges P. Drouillard. (Mr. Schroll grew up in the Maumee region of Ohio and was familiar with the history of the Shawnees of that region. Other clues subsequently confirmed his accurate knowledge. Colleen and Allen Schroll specialize in supplying materials and finished products pertinent to understanding and re-enacting the colonial and early federal periods in North American history.)

Thanks also to Mrs. Jane Randol Jackson of Cape Girardeau, who pointed me in the direction of other information relative to old documents dealing with the Indians of Cape Girardeau County, especially the Absentee Shawnees, of which "Drewyer" was a part. Also thanks for providing a critique of the manuscript in draft.

Gratitude also to the Missouri Historical Society of St. Louis, Mo., for granting permission to publish copies of old documents in their possession bearing the signatures of Georges P. Drouillard, which may help to give us insights into his life and times.

Additional thanks go to Mr. Corey Scott of TiCor Graphics, Jefferson City, Mo., for cover design and suggestions, as well as to my wife and sons for their help with manuscript and photos, as well as putting up with my re-enacting rôle of Georges "Drewyer." It is by the process of re-enacting that the historian gets to fully appreciate the real hardships endured by the pioneers of American history.

Special thanks go to those who were willing to be included in the presentation of fine dining establishments along the Missouri River. Also I thank the late Hendrik Van Loon, author of *The Story of Mankind* [Garden City, N.Y., the Garden City Publishing Co., Inc. © 1921, 1926, and 1938] for including the admonition, "What is the use of a book without pictures?" He inspired this author to include maps, photos and drawings.

We appreciate all those authors who have written earlier books, so that we all can learn about our predecessors in history. Sometimes the only reason we can get it right is by comparing what others have had to say. Many are listed among the references. Thanks!

About the Author

Richard M. Gaffney earned his B.A. and M.A. degrees in American History at the University of Maine, Orono, Maine.

Born in Maine, Mr. Gaffney had a grandfather, Joseph DeGagné, who was born on an island in the St. Lawrence River in the Province of Québec, Canada. In the 19th Century, Mr. DeGagné and his brother, Georges, sailed by sloop down the St. Lawrence River and then north to the coast of Labrador, where they engaged in trading with the Indians of that region. He shared those stories with his grandson, many years later, in the mid-20th Century.

Mr. Gaffney had a grandmother, whom he called *Nokomis* ("my grandmother" in Wabanaki Indian language), and who related to him tales of growing up on an island on the coast of Maine, where the Penobscot Indians fished and sold woven ash baskets to the summer people. Mr. Gaffney later lived among the Wabanaki people and learned some of the language. He took his French and Indian roots and his historian's skills, and became an author and historical re-enactor over many decades.

In 1975, Mr. Gaffney was one of many re-enactors who followed Col. Benedict Arnold's famous March to Québec in the autumn of 1775. He and Mrs. Gaffney and their children marched in parade in Boston, Massachusetts, on the occasion of the visit of Queen Elizabeth II of Great Britain in 1976. He also participated in the re-enactment of the famed Battle of Bennington of 1777. The family moved to Missouri in 1979.

Now an elder of the native people, Mr. Gaffney brings his understanding and appreciation of his French Canadian and Algonquian Indian roots to bear in his portrayal of Georges P. Drouillard, the famous Shawnee and Canadian hunter and interpreter of the Lewis and Clark Expedition of Northwest Discovery.

A member of the State Historical Society of Missouri, the Discovery Expedition of St. Charles, the Jefferson City Lewis and Clark Bicentennial Task Force, and the Manitou Bluffs Mid-Missouri Chapter of the Lewis and Clark Trail Heritage Foundation, Mr. Gaffney did research on his subject, Georges Pierre Drouillard, prior to undertaking the production of this book.

Mr. Gaffney is married to the former Dolores Ann Walker, of Cherokee descent, born in Muskogee, Oklahoma (a real "Okie from Muskogee.") They have four grown children, and are active in Boy Scouts, as well as Lewis and Clark commemorations. Mrs. Gaffney also is a noted seamstress.

George P. Drouillard (portrayed by R.M. Gaffney) and White Dove (Mrs. Dolores Gaffney), on the grounds of Locust Grove, east of Louisville, Ky., autumn, 2003, at the time of the Falls of the Ohio signature event of the Lewis and Clark Bicentennial Commemoration.
(Photo by Gerald D. Manchester.)

Also by Richard M. Gaffney

Compiler and Editor, **The Comprehensive Plan**, Utica, N.Y.: Herkimer-Oneida Counties Comprehensive Planning Program, 1970.

With Nat Rutstein, **A Vital Resource, Agriculture in Hampshire County**, Northampton, Mass.: Hampshire County Planning Department, 1976.

Out of Harm's Way, A Flood Damage Reduction Plan for the Lower Meramec River Valley in Missouri, St. Paul, Minn.: Upper Mississippi River Basin Commission (UMRBC), 1980.

Flood Report Analysis, Water Resources Report Number 54, Rolla, Missouri: Missouri Department of Natural Resources, Division of Geology and Land Survey, 1996. [Re. the Great Flood of 1993 in Missouri, a comparison of the recommendations of numerous post-flood reports by various agencies.]

"Swamped with Success," in **Missouri Resources**, Volume 16, Number 2, Missouri Department of Natural Resources, Jefferson City, Mo., Summer, 1999, pp. 2-5. [Re. Adaptive use of wetland resources on private lands.]

With Charles Hays, William J. Bryan IV, and Amy E. Randles, **A Summary of Missouri Water Laws**, Water Resources Report Number 51, Missouri State Water Plan Series Volume VII, Rolla, Missouri: Missouri Department of Natural Resources, Division of Geology and Land Survey, and Jefferson City: Office of Missouri Attorney General Jay Nixon, 2000. [Missouri Statutory and Case Law relative to water and water resources; mentions federal laws only in passing.]

"North American Colonial Calendars," in ***Muzzle Blasts***, Vol. 67, No. 8, National Muzzle Loading Rifle Association, Friendship, Indiana: April, 2006. [Re. the switch from the Julian Calendar to the Gregorian Calendar in A.D. 1754.]

Information about the Shawnees

"As early as 1793, a group of conservative Shawnees took possession of a 625-square-mile land grant from the Spanish government. The tract lay south of St. Louis on the west side of the Mississippi River near Cape Girardeau.

"By 1815, some of the Shawnees who had relocated there moved west again to Arkansas and Oklahoma. By 1824, about 800 Shawnees still lived in Ohio, while 1,383 Shawnees were recorded as living in Missouri.

"In 1825, a treaty ceded all the Shawnees' Missouri lands to the United States in exchange for land in Kansas.

"Following the War Between the States, the Shawnees of Kansas were forced to move to Oklahoma Indian Territory and accept citizenship in the Cherokee Nation. They then became known as the Cherokee Shawnees, distinguishing them from the Eastern Shawnees and the Absentee Shawnees.

"It took until the year 2000 to get the Congress and the President to enact the Shawnee Tribe Status Act, which separated the Shawnees from the Cherokees and restored the Shawnees to their position as a legally recognized Indian tribe."

Source: The Missouri Lewis and Clark Bicentennial Commission, *American Indian Resource Handbook*, 2004, p. 39.

The Absentee Shawnee Tribe of Indians of Oklahoma,
2025 South Gordon Cooper Drive,
Shawnee, OK 74801; Dial 405:275-4030; Population 3,004.
[This appears to be the tribe that has descended from Chief Kishkalwa's Band of Shawnees that lived near Cape Girardeau, Missouri, the band of which Georges P. Drouillard was a member.]

The Shawnee Tribe (formerly the "Cherokee Shawnees"),
P.O. Box 189,
Miami OK 74355; Dial 918:542-2441.
www.shawnee-tribe.org

Eastern Shawnee Tribe of Oklahoma (also called the "Loyal Shawnees"),
P.O. Box 350,
Seneca, MO 64865; Dial 918:666-2435.
www.easternshawnee.org

Shawnee Nation, United Remnant Band,
P.O. Box 162,
Dayton, Ohio, 45401-0162; Dial 937:592-9592.
www.shawneeurb.homestead.com
    Source: Hawk Pope, *Shawnee Nation, United Remnant Band*, 2000.

About the Book

Bon Appetit! -- When Georges Drouillard, the hired civilian hunter and interpreter, accompanied Captains Lewis and Clark on their Voyage of Discovery, 1803-1806, there were <u>no</u> "fine dining establishments" along the Mississippi River!

Today, there <u>are</u>, and Part I of this book provides travelers of the Lewis and Clark Trail guidance to some of the best in both fine dining and "trailside fare."

Called "Drewyer" in the *Journals* of Lewis and Clark, this adept hunter was also a valued interpreter for the expedition. Few people know that he was a Shawnee man whose residence was in the area of Cape Girardeau, Missouri, both before and after the famous journey to the Pacific Ocean.

In Part II of the book, **The Life and Times of Georges P. Drouillard**, readers learn more about the historical, cultural, and geographic context of this man, Drewyer, who deserves to be better known and appreciated.

YOU are invited to come along for the ride. **Enjoy!**

Printed in the United States
58243LVS00002BA/574-645